TEAM SPIRIT ®

SMART BOOKS FOR YOUNG FANS

THE ARIZONA DIAMONDBACKS

BY
MARK STEWART

NORWOOD HOUSE PRESS
CHICAGO, ILLINOIS

Norwood House Press
P.O. Box 316598
Chicago, Illinois 60631

For information regarding Norwood House Press, please visit our website at:
www.norwoodhousepress.com or call 866-565-2900.

All photos courtesy of Getty Images except the following:
Black Book Partners Archives (6, 9, 35 top, 36, 43 both), The Sporting News (7), Tom DiPace (10, 11, 14, 31),
Topps, Inc. (15, 23, 29, 37, 41, 42 top & bottom left, 45), SportsChrome (25, 36),
Arizona Diamondbacks (33), Matt Richman (48).
Cover Photo: Christian Petersen/Getty Images

The memorabilia and artifacts pictured in this book are presented for educational and informational purposes,
and come from the collection of the author.

Editor: Mike Kennedy
Designer: Ron Jaffe
Project Management: Black Book Partners, LLC.
Special thanks to Topps, Inc.

Library of Congress Cataloging-in-Publication Data

Stewart, Mark, 1960-
  The Arizona Diamondbacks / by Mark Stewart.
      p. cm. -- (Team spirit)
  Includes bibliographical references and index.
  Summary: "A Team Spirit Baseball edition featuring the Arizona
Diamondbacks that chronicles the history and accomplishments of the team.
Includes access to the Team Spirit website which provides additional
information and photos"--Provided by publisher.

  ISBN 978-1-59953-472-5 (library edition : alk. paper) -- ISBN
1-59953-472-X (library edition : alk. paper) -- ISBN 978-1-60357-352-8
(ebook) -- ISBN 1-60357-352-6 (ebook) 1. Arizona Diamondbacks (Baseball
team)--History--Juvenile literature. I. Title.
  GV875.A64S74 2012
  796.357'640979173--dc23
                                                    2011047756

Manufactured in the United States of America in North Mankato, Minnesota.
196N—012012

COVER PHOTO: The Diamondbacks are a picture of joy after a win in 2011.

TABLE OF CONTENTS

ABOUT OUR GLOSSARY

In this book, there may be several words that you are reading for the first time. Some are sports words, some are new vocabulary words, and some are familiar words that are used in an unusual way. All of these words are defined on page 46. Throughout the book, sports words appear in **bold type**. Regular vocabulary words appear in ***bold italic type***.

MEET THE DIAMONDBACKS

The best sports teams are the ones with a winning *tradition*. In baseball, it can take many *decades* to build a club that's a *contender*. The Arizona Diamondbacks decided to do things a little differently. They didn't play their first season until 1998, but they put an exciting team on the field right away.

Is Arizona an impatient team? Not at all. The club's coaches and fans show great patience with their young players. When the Diamondbacks make mistakes on the field, they learn from them. That is a big part of the team's success.

This book tells the story of the Diamondbacks. Like the snake that they are named after, the "D-backs" are coiled to strike at any time. No opponent wants to stir them. And no lead is safe until the final out is made.

Chris Young gets a warm welcome from teammates after a home run. Arizona's patience with young players has paid off time and again.

GLORY DAYS

The story of the Arizona Diamondbacks begins in 1995. That year, baseball owners decided to add two new teams for the 1998 season. The Tampa Bay Devil Rays (now known as the Rays) joined the **American League (AL)**. The Diamondbacks joined the **National League (NL)**.

The Diamondbacks were named after a species of rattlesnake that lives in the deserts of the American Southwest. The team's main owner was Jerry Colangelo. He also owned the Phoenix Suns basketball team. Colangelo's partners included Phillip Knight, who owned Nike, comedian Billy Crystal, and basketball star Danny Manning. The D-backs struggled in their first season and finished last in the **NL West**. Their best players were Matt Williams, Jay Bell, Devon White, and Andy Benes.

Arizona fans were willing to be patient with the Diamondbacks, but the owners were eager to win right away. Over the winter, they added pitcher Randy Johnson and a whole new outfield of Luis Gonzalez, Steve Finley, and Tony Womack. The Diamondbacks won 100 games in just their second season—something no **expansion team** had ever done.

Over the next two seasons, Arizona welcomed more experienced stars, including Mark Grace, Reggie Sanders, Craig Counsell, Curt Schilling, and Miguel Batista. In 2001, the Diamondbacks captured the **pennant**. Johnson went 21–6 and won the **Cy Young Award**. Gonzalez also had an amazing year. He hit 57 home runs and had 142 **runs batted in (RBIs)**.

LEFT: Luis Gonzales gets ready to hit.
ABOVE: Jay Bell was a star for Arizona in its early years.

The Diamondbacks faced the New York Yankees in the 2001 **World Series**. With America recovering from the shock and sadness of the September 11 terrorist attacks, fans nationwide enjoyed the *diversion* that baseball provided. The series lasted seven dramatic games. Arizona won the championship in the last inning of the final game. Johnson and Schilling shared

honors as the series **Most Valuable Player (MVP)**. With their title, the Diamondbacks reminded fans that playing hard and having fun was a great recipe for victory.

The Diamondbacks won the NL West again in 2002, but they did not return to the World Series. Over the next few years, the team brought in more top stars, including Shawn Green, Russ Ortiz, Orlando Hudson, and Troy Glaus. Unfortunately, age and injuries kept the Diamondbacks from reaching the **playoffs** again until 2007. By then, Arizona had rebuilt its team around a group

LEFT: Randy Johnson peers in at a hitter.   **ABOVE**: *The Sporting News* picked Curt Schilling as its 2001 Sportsman of the Year.

of young hitters. They included Stephen Drew, Conor Jackson, Chris Young, Miguel Montero, Mark Reynolds, and Justin Upton. The team's top pitchers were Brandon Webb and Jose Valverde.

Arizona fans expected great things from this group. Yet as often happens in sports, the Diamondbacks took a step backwards instead. Webb suffered an arm injury, and the young hitters did not improve as quickly as the team had hoped. Arizona went through losing seasons in 2009 and 2010. During that time, the D-backs rebuilt their club for the future.

By 2011, the Diamondbacks were back on the winning track. Ryan Roberts, Aaron Hill, Paul Goldschmidt, Daniel Hudson, and Ian Kennedy helped Arizona

play exciting baseball all season long. Again, the Diamondbacks showed that amazing things can happen when a team refuses to give up. No matter how far behind the D-backs were in a game, they fought hard for nine innings. At season's end, Arizona was the NL West champion again—and more than half of the team's wins were thrilling comebacks!

LEFT: Brandon Webb led the NL in wins twice.
ABOVE: Daniel Hudson

HOME TURF

The Diamondbacks have played in the same stadium since they joined the NL in 1998. It was only the second ballpark in baseball with a **retractable** roof. Summer days are very hot in Arizona. The Diamondbacks keep the roof open until a few hours before game time to give the grass sunlight. They close the roof to let the air conditioning cool the stadium. Each game, a few lucky fans can also beat the heat by jumping into the swimming pool located behind the right field wall.

Another notable feature of Arizona's stadium is the center field wall. It stands 25 feet tall, so hitting home runs over it is not easy. A huge video scoreboard hangs above the fence.

BY THE NUMBERS

- The Diamondbacks' stadium has 48,633 seats.
- The distance from home plate to the left field foul pole is 330 feet.
- The distance from home plate to the center field fence is 407 feet.
- The distance from home plate to the right field foul pole is 334 feet.

The roof is open at the D-backs stadium for a 2007 playoff game.

DRESSED FOR SUCCESS

For their first nine seasons, the Diamondbacks used three main colors—blue, brown, and purple. The blue was a shade called turquoise, which is a beautiful stone found in Arizona. The brown was meant to represent copper. Arizona is the nation's top copper producer. The purple was the same color worn by the Phoenix Suns basketball team.

In 2007, the Diamondbacks unveiled a new uniform and changed its main colors to Sedona Red and Sonora Sand. Sedona is the name of an Arizona city that is surrounded by beautiful red rocks. Sonora is the name of a desert in the state.

Arizona's *logo* features the letter *A*. The team uses a rattlesnake symbol on its cap. It is shaped like the letter *D*, for Diamondbacks.

LEFT: Ian Kennedy wears the team's 2011 road jersey.   **ABOVE**: Gregg Olson wears the team's purple uniform on his 1998 trading card.

WE WON!

When it comes to winning a World Series, a team must have experienced players. That wasn't a problem for the Diamondbacks in 2001. They had plenty of *veterans* on the team. However, only one had won a championship. But the D-backs were hungry for a World Series ring. Manager Bob Brenly worked hard to turn that hunger into an actual championship. It would not be easy.

In the first round of the playoffs, the Diamondbacks battled the St. Louis Cardinals down to the last inning of the fifth and final game. Curt Schilling had already pitched a **shutout** in Game 1. Now he was back on the mound for Game 5. The contest went into the bottom of the ninth inning tied 1–1. The Diamondbacks scored the winning run on a bloop single by Tony Womack.

Next up were the Atlanta Braves in the **National League Championship Series (NLCS)**. In a duel between baseball's best pitching staffs, the Diamondbacks came out on top, four games to one. Schilling and Miguel Batista each recorded a victory, and Randy Johnson won two times to lead Arizona to its first pennant.

The World Series matched Arizona against the New York Yankees. The Diamondbacks won the first two games in front of their home fans. Johnson and Schilling gave up a total of one run, while their teammates scored 13 times. For once, it looked like the D-backs might have it easy.

The series moved to New York, where the Yankees felt very confident. They won Game 3 by a score of 2–1. In Game 4, Schilling was cruising along with a two-run lead when Brenly decided to remove him. The Diamondbacks were stunned when Byung-Hyun Kim gave up home runs to Tino Martinez and Derek Jeter to

LEFT: Curt Schilling delivers a pitch in the 2001 playoffs.
ABOVE: Randy Johnson thanks the heavens after winning Game 2 of the World Series.

17

lose the game in the 10th inning. The next night, Kim was called in again to protect a two-run lead. This time, he gave up a game-tying home run to Scott Brosius. The Yankees won in the 12th inning.

The teams returned to Arizona to finish the series. The Diamondbacks had to win twice. In Game 6, they got 22 hits and destroyed the Yankees, 15–2. Some fans were worried that the Arizona offense might struggle the following night in Game 7. At first, it looked that way.

Schilling and Roger Clemens of the Yankees pitched brilliantly. The Diamondbacks got one run in the sixth inning, but New York scored in the seventh and eighth to take a 2–1 lead. The Yankees then sent Mariano Rivera to the mound. He was the best relief pitcher in baseball.

The Diamondbacks would not back down. Mark Grace led off the ninth with a single to center field. David Dellucci replaced him as a pinch-runner. Damian Miller bunted, and Rivera made a bad throw to second. Dellucci was safe. Next up was Jay Bell, who also bunted. This time, Rivera pounced off the mound and threw out Dellucci at third base.

Womack walked to the plate next for Arizona. Brenly let him swing away. Womack responded with a double to tie the score at 2–2. With runners on second and third, Rivera hit Craig Counsell with a pitch to load the bases.

Into the batter's box stepped Luis Gonzalez. The fans in Arizona rose to their feet. The stadium had never been noisier. Rivera's second pitch was a fastball that darted to the inside corner of home plate. Gonzalez swung, and the ball climbed softly in the air and floated over Jeter's head at shortstop. Bell came home with the winning run. The Diamondbacks were world champions!

LEFT: Tony Womack contributed three hits to Arizona's victory in Game 6.
RIGHT: Luis Gonzalez celebrates his winning hit in Game 7.

GO-TO GUYS

To be a true star in baseball, you need more than a quick bat and a strong arm. You have to be a "go-to guy"—someone the manager wants on the pitcher's mound or in the batter's box when it matters most. Fans of the Diamondbacks have had a lot to cheer about over the years, including these great stars …

THE PIONEERS

JAY BELL   Second Baseman/Shortstop
• BORN: 12/11/1965   • PLAYED FOR TEAM: 1998 TO 2002

Jay Bell was one of the friendliest, smartest players in the game. Bell set an example for Arizona's younger stars. In 1999, he hit 38 home runs and became an **All-Star**.

LUIS GONZALEZ   Outfielder
• BORN: 9/3/1967   • PLAYED FOR TEAM: 1999 TO 2006

Luis Gonzalez was a good hitter during his first 10 years in the **big leagues**. He became a great one after he joined the Diamondbacks. "Gonzo" led the NL in hits in 1999 and smashed 57 home runs in 2001.

STEVE FINLEY   Outfielder

- BORN: 3/12/1965
- PLAYED FOR TEAM: 1999 TO 2004

Steve Finley was another experienced star who loved playing in Arizona. Finley hit 69 home runs for the D-backs in his first two seasons, and he also played excellent defense in center field.

RANDY JOHNSON   Pitcher

- BORN: 9/10/1963
- PLAYED FOR TEAM: 1999 TO 2004 & 2007 TO 2008

Randy Johnson was the greatest pitcher in Arizona history. The "Big Unit" led the NL in strikeouts five times and won the Cy Young Award in each of his first four seasons with the team. In 2001, Johnson struck out 20 batters in a game.

CURT SCHILLING   Pitcher

- BORN: 11/14/1966   • PLAYED FOR TEAM: 2000 TO 2003

Arizona traded four young players to get Curt Schilling. He was worth the price. Schilling won 22 games in 2001 and had four more victories in the playoffs and World Series. In 2002, he and Randy Johnson became the first teammates to each strike out 300 batters in the same season.

ABOVE: Steve Finley

JOSE VALVERDE   Pitcher

- BORN: 3/24/1979
- PLAYED FOR TEAM: 2003 TO 2007

Jose Valverde was one of the best relief pitchers in baseball from the moment he joined the Diamondbacks. In 2007, after recovering from an arm injury, he **saved** 47 games.

BRANDON WEBB   Pitcher

- BORN: 5/9/1979
- PLAYED FOR TEAM: 2003 TO 2009

Brandon Webb used a great sinking fastball to become Arizona's best pitcher. In 2006, he tied for the NL lead in wins and shutouts, and won the Cy Young Award. Two years later, he topped the league in wins again.

MIGUEL MONTERO   Catcher

- BORN: 7/9/1983   • FIRST YEAR WITH TEAM: 2006

The Diamondbacks signed Miguel Montero when he was a teenager. He was already a good hitter, but it took time for him to learn how to be a big-league catcher. Ten years later, Montero became an All-Star.

ABOVE: Jose Valverde   **RIGHT**: Daniel Hudson

CHRIS YOUNG   Outfielder

- BORN: 9/5/1983 • FIRST YEAR WITH TEAM: 2006

The Diamondbacks traded for Chris Young hoping that he would become a slugger. In his first full season in Arizona, he hit 32 home runs and stole 27 bases. Young was picked for the **All-Star Game** in 2010.

JUSTIN UPTON   Outfielder

- BORN: 8/25/1987 • FIRST YEAR WITH TEAM: 2007

Justin Upton helped the Diamondbacks win the NL West in 2007 at the age of 19. In 2011, Upton developed into Arizona's best player. He led the team with 31 homers and 105 runs, and also stole 21 bases.

DANIEL HUDSON   Pitcher

- BORN: 3/9/1987

- FIRST YEAR WITH TEAM: 2010

When Arizona traded for Daniel Hudson during the 2010 season, few fans knew who he was. He introduced himself by losing just one game the rest of the way. In 2011, Hudson won 16 games and teamed with Ian Kennedy to give the Diamondbacks two aces.

CALLING THE SHOTS

Throughout their history, the Diamondbacks have shown how a good manager can make a team better. Their first manager was Buck Showalter. He had helped build the championship teams of the New York Yankees during the 1990s. Under Showalter, the Diamondbacks won 100 games in just their second year.

In 2001, Bob Brenly took over and became only the third manager ever to win the World Series in his first season. He had been a power-hitting catcher as a player. Arizona's hitters felt that they had a lot in common with him. Brenly was also very good working with his pitchers.

The team's next manager was Bob Melvin. He had also been a big-league catcher and was one of Brenly's assistant coaches in 2001. Melvin picked up where Brenly left off. The Diamondbacks finished first in the NL West in 2007, and Melvin was named Manager of the Year.

In the years that followed, Arizona decided to rebuild the team. They lost a lot of games, but they learned from their mistakes. Midway through the 2010 season, Kirk Gibson was promoted

Bob Brenly won a championship in his first season with the Diamondbacks.

from coach to manager. The Diamondbacks went 34–49 the rest of the year.

Many wondered if Gibson was ready to manage in the big leagues. In 2011, he proved that he was. Gibson had been the NL MVP in 1988. He knew how to inspire his young players. He also knew how to give older players new confidence. At the end of the year, the Diamondbacks were NL West champs again.

Whenever Randy Johnson pitched for the Diamondbacks, there was always a chance that he would treat fans to a truly special performance. That is one of the reasons why a crowd of more than 20,000 showed up at Turner Field in Atlanta on a Tuesday night in May of 2004.

The Diamondbacks were in a rebuilding year. They would lose 111 games during the season. Outside of Johnson, there was not much to see. But Braves fans still got their money's worth that night. Inning after inning, Johnson set down the opposing hitters in order. Most of the Braves had two strikes on them before they knew it. Johnson struck out 13 Atlanta batters in all.

Johnson's fastball got stronger as the game went on. His curve and **slider** were bending sharply as they reached home plate. The closest Atlanta came to a hit was a weak grounder by its pitcher, Mike Hampton. Alex Cintron scooped up the roller, and his throw to first arrived a half-step before Hampton.

The D-backs congratulate Randy Johnson after his perfect game.

The 27th batter for the Braves was Eddie Perez. Johnson struck him out with a blazing fastball. It was a **perfect game**— only the 16th in history. Johnson pumped his fist and celebrated as his teammates surrounded him on the mound. The Atlanta fans gave him a standing ovation as he walked into the dugout.

At age 40, Johnson was the oldest pitcher to throw a perfect game. The record had been held by 37-year-old Cy Young. Johnson knew something about that baseball legend. He had five Cy Young Awards in his trophy case.

"This is one of those nights where a superior athlete was on top of his game," said Arizona manager Bob Brenly. "There was a tremendous rhythm out there. His focus, his concentration, his stuff—everything was as good as it could possibly be."

LEGEND HAS IT

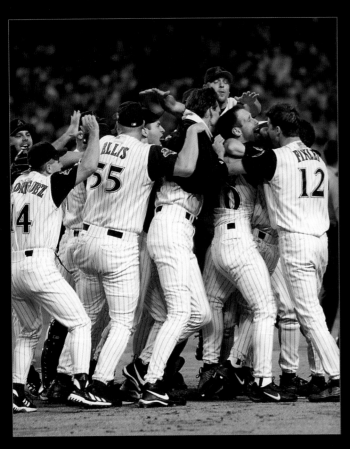

LEGEND HAS IT that it was. When the Diamondbacks came to bat in the bottom of the ninth inning of Game 7, they trailed the New York Yankees by one run. No team had ever been in that situation in the World Series and won. Arizona scored twice to take the championship. Facing the great Mariano Rivera, the D-backs found a way to push the tying and winning runs across home plate. At the start of the inning, they were three outs away from defeat. They walked off the field as champions.

ABOVE: The Diamondbacks celebrate after their history-making comeback.
RIGHT: Justin Upton

LEGEND HAS IT that Kirk Gibson was. Gibson is a licensed pilot. He once set a world record for flying a Cessna 206 propeller plane at 25,200 feet, which is almost five miles high. The old record was 22,000 feet. Gibson broke it in 1987, and no one has flown higher since.

WHO WAS THE MOST-BRUISED DIAMONDBACK?

LEGEND HAS IT that Justin Upton was. In 2011, Upton became one of baseball's best power hitters. Pitchers hoped to make him flinch by throwing fastballs close to his body on the inside part of home plate. Upton refused to give in—and he had the bruises to prove it. The young outfielder was hit by a pitch 19 times. Andy Fox, who was "plunked" 18 times in 1998, had held the old team record. No one in the big leagues was hit more often than Upton in 2011.

JUSTIN UPTON
Outfield

Arizona Diamondbacks®

Before every baseball season, the experts try to predict where each team will finish. Often there is great disagreement. But during the spring of 2011, everyone agreed on one thing: Arizona would finish in last place in the NL West.

Manager Kirk Gibson had many problems to solve as the season started. Several of his pitchers were hurt. Others lacked experience. Gibson wasn't sure who would play first base or third base. He didn't know who would hit at the top of the batting order. The Diamondbacks' sluggers—Kelly Johnson, Chris Young, and Justin Upton—all struck out too much. As for Gibson himself, he had only managed part of one season. What a mess!

Luckily for the Diamondbacks and their fans, a baseball season is not played on paper. After struggling for a month or so, the team began to play with confidence. Ryan Roberts was given a chance to play every day. He hit home runs and stole bases like an All-Star. Paul Goldschmidt took over at first base and did a great job. Aaron Hill became the new second baseman in August and hit better than .300. And Upton turned into a great **clutch** hitter at the age of 23.

J.J. Putz had a lot to smile about during the 2011 season.

The team's young pitchers also stepped up and showed they were ready to win close games. Ian Kennedy, Daniel Hudson, and Josh Collmenter combined for a record of 47–26. At the age of 34, relief pitcher J.J. Putz was the "old man" of the staff. He had a great year with 45 saves.

In the middle of August, the Diamondbacks won seven games in a row to take over first place in the NL West. Then they lost six in a row. The experts predicted Arizona's season would soon be over. Once again, however, they had counted out the D-backs too soon. Arizona won its next nine games and never looked back. The Diamondbacks ended up going from worst to first and won the NL West by eight games.

TEAM SPIRIT

Every baseball team promises its fans that it will build a winner. Keeping that promise can be a challenge. The Diamondbacks won the World Series in their fourth season, and the fans love them for it. Of course, no team can have a winning record every single year. But even during seasons when the losses piled up and the future looked dim, Arizona worked to add winning players to its lineup. The fans knew they wouldn't have to wait long to root for a contender.

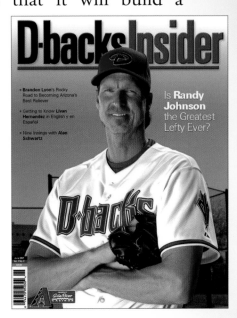

The Diamondbacks say *thank you* to their fans in many ways. The coolest way? That would be the swimming pool behind the fence in right field. It can get pretty warm on summer nights in Arizona. Win or lose, the people watching the game from this section enjoy an unforgettable night at the ballpark.

LEFT: Fans stay cool in the D-backs' pool.
ABOVE: The team stays in the news by publishing its own magazine.

TIMELINE

Steve Finley

1999
Steve Finley becomes the first Diamondback to win a Gold Glove.

2001
Arizona defeats the New York Yankees to win the World Series.

1998
The Diamondbacks play their first season.

2000
Tony Womack leads the league with 14 triples.

Buck Showalter was Arizona's first manager.

Tony Womack

Brandon Webb delivers a pitch during his Cy Young season.

2004
Randy Johnson pitches a perfect game.

2006
Brandon Webb wins the Cy Young Award.

2011
Arizona wins the NL West again.

2002
Randy Johnson leads the NL in wins, strikeouts, and **earned run average (ERA)**.

2007
The Diamondbacks win the NL West for the fourth time.

Randy Johnson

The D-backs celebrate their 2007 title.

Going, Going, Gonzo!

One of the hardest things to do as a hitter is to finish the year with 100 extra-base hits (doubles, triples, and home runs). In 2001, Luis Gonzalez hit 57 homers, 36 doubles, and seven triples to record exactly 100.

Breakfast Club

On the day tickets for Arizona's first game went on sale in January of 1998, they were gone by lunchtime.

K Factor

In 2002, Randy Johnson became the first pitcher to reach 300 strikeouts (or "Ks") in a season five times in a row.

THANKS FOR THE MEMORIES

In 2010, Edwin Jackson pitched the second **no-hitter** in team history. Five weeks later, he was traded away. One of the players Arizona got in the deal was Daniel Hudson, who won 16 games in 2011.

CHEAP SEATS

For many years, the Diamondbacks were famous for offering fans the best bargain in baseball—$1 seats. They finally raised the price in 2007.

TRIPLE THREAT

The first D-back to lead the league in a major category was David Dellucci. He hit an NL-best 12 triples in 1998.

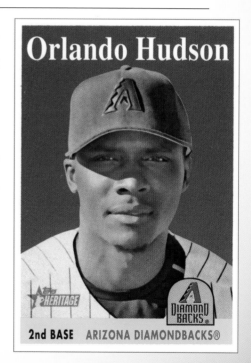

GOOD AS GOLD

In 2006, Orlando Hudson won a Gold Glove for his excellent fielding with the Diamondbacks. He had already won the award with the Toronto Blue Jays in the AL. Hudson was just the sixth player to be a "gold glover" in both the AL and NL.

LEFT: Luis Gonzalez   **ABOVE**: Orlando Hudson

TALKING BASEBALL

"You could just feel that it was a team that had a chance to do something special."

▶ **BOB BRENLY**, *ON THE CLUB HE TOOK OVER IN 2001*

"I've had personal accomplishments before, but nothing feels better than a group of guys coming together with one goal and achieving that goal."

▶ **JUSTIN UPTON**, *ON THE IMPORTANCE OF PUTTING TEAM GOALS BEFORE INDIVIDUAL GOALS*

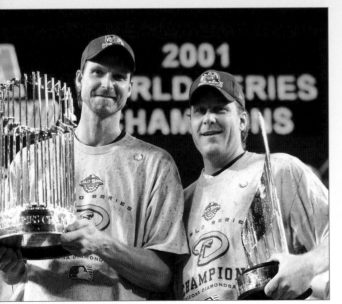

"I expect to win. I've never been content with anything I've ever done."

▶ **RANDY JOHNSON**, *ON THE ATTITUDE THAT HELPED HIM BECOME ONE OF BASEBALL'S GREATEST PITCHERS EVER*

"A lot of the guys don't ever get the opportunity to play in the playoffs or a World Series. So I feel very fortunate to have reached this accomplishment."

▶ **LUIS GONZALEZ**, ON ARIZONA'S CHAMPIONSHIP IN 2001

"He's very confident. And why shouldn't he be? He's got great stuff."

▶ **KIRK GIBSON**, ON IAN KENNEDY, WHO WON 21 GAMES IN 2011

"The most important thing about playing baseball is to have fun."

▶ **MARK GRACE**, ON WHAT DROVE HIM AS A PLAYER

"That's a good thing about being a catcher. If you don't show results as a hitter, you can show results by helping your pitchers."

▶ **MIGUEL MONTERO**, ON WHY HE FOCUSES AS MUCH ON DEFENSE AS HE DOES ON OFFENSE

LEFT: Randy Johnson poses with Curt Schilling after the 2001 World Series.
ABOVE: Mark Grace

GREAT DEBATES

People who root for the Diamondbacks love to compare their favorite moments, teams, and players. Some debates have been going on for years! How would you settle these classic baseball arguments?

THE 2011 DIAMONDBACKS WERE BASEBALL'S 'COMEBACK KINGS' ...

... because they came from behind to win 48 times—more than any other team. No lead was safe against Arizona. They had great clutch hitters, including Luis Gonzalez, Mark Grace, and Reggie Sanders (LEFT). Arizona trailed by six runs to the Houston Astros twice and won both games. The Diamondbacks also beat the Los Angeles Dodgers when they were behind 6–1 in the 10th inning.

THE 2001 D-BACKS DESERVE THE COMEBACK CROWN ...

... because they did something no team had ever done before. In Game 7 of the World Series that year, Arizona went into the bottom of the 9th inning behind by a run. The D-backs scored twice to win the championship. They beat Mariano Rivera, the king of all relief pitchers. That makes the 2001 Diamondbacks the greatest comeback kings.

BRANDON WEBB WAS THE TEAM'S BEST HOME-GROWN' PLAYER ...

.. because he was one of baseball's best pitchers three years in a row. A home-grown player is someone who is signed by a team and then trained in the **minors**. From 2006 to 2008, Webb won 56 games for Arizona. He led the NL in games started, games won, and shutouts twice. It was very hard to score runs against Webb—and almost impossible to hit a home run against him. He won the Cy Young Award in 2006 and was runner-up in 2007 and 2008.

NO WAY! JUSTIN UPTON WAS THE BEST PLAYER TO COME UP THROUGH THE MINORS FOR ARIZONA ...

JUSTIN **UPTON**
ARIZONA DIAMONDBACKS® OF

.. because he helped the team win every day. A good pitcher appears in only 30 to 35 games a year. In 2011, Upton played in 159 games and came to bat almost 700 times. Arizona's opponents had to worry about Upton (RIGHT) all the time, and he gave them plenty to worry about. He had 75 extra-base hits during the year and drove in runs when the Diamondbacks needed them most.

The great Diamondbacks teams and players have left their marks on the record books. These are the "best of the best" ...

Curt Schilling

DIAMONDBACKS AWARD WINNERS

WINNER	AWARD	YEAR
Randy Johnson	Cy Young Award	1999
Randy Johnson	Cy Young Award	2000
Randy Johnson	Cy Young Award	2001
Craig Counsell	NLCS MVP	2001
Curt Schilling	World Series co-MVP	2001
Randy Johnson	World Series co-MVP	2001
Randy Johnson	Cy Young Award	2002
Brandon Webb	Cy Young Award	2006
Bob Melvin	Manager of the Year	2007
Kirk Gibson	Manager of the Year	2011

Brandon Webb

Mark Grace hugs
NLCS MVP Craig Counsell.

ACHIEVEMENT	YEAR
NL West Champions	1999
NL West Champions	2001
NL Pennant Winners	2001
World Series Champions	2001
NL West Champions	2002
NL West Champions	2007
NL West Champions	2011

ABOVE: Conor Jackson hit .284 for the 2007 team.
LEFT: Eric Byrnes led the 2007 D-backs in hits, runs, and stolen bases.

PINPOINTS

The history of a baseball team is made up of many smaller stories. These stories take place all over the map—not just in the city a team calls "home." Match the pushpins on these maps to the **TEAM FACTS**, and you will begin to see the story of the Diamondbacks unfold!

1 Phoenix, Arizona—*The team has played here since 1998.*

2 Walnut Creek, California—*Randy Johnson was born here.*

3 Houston, Texas—*Chris Young was born here.*

4 La Crosse, Wisconsin—*Damian Miller was born here.*

5 Ashland, Kentucky—*Brandon Webb was born here.*

6 Chatham, Virginia—*Tony Womack was born here.*

7 New York, New York—*The Diamondbacks played in the 2001 World Series here.*

8 Denver, Colorado—*The Diamondbacks played in the 2007 NLCS here.*

9 Tampa, Florida—*Luis Gonzalez was born here.*

10 Anchorage, Alaska—*Curt Schilling was born here.*

11 Caracas, Distrito Federal, Venezuela—*Miguel Montero was born here.*

12 Kwangju, South Korea—*Byung-Hyun Kim was born here.*

Miguel Montero

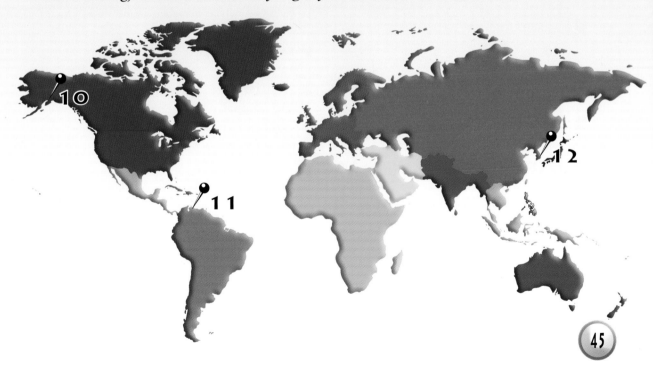

45

GLOSSARY

🧠 **ALL-STAR**—A player who is selected to play in baseball's annual All-Star Game.

🧠 **ALL-STAR GAME**—Baseball's annual game featuring the best players from the American League and National League.

🧠 **AMERICAN LEAGUE (AL)**—One of baseball's two major leagues; the AL began play in 1901.

🧠 **BIG LEAGUES**—The top level of professional baseball.

🧠 **CLUTCH**—Pressure situations.

🧠 *CONTENDER*—A team that competes for a championship.

🧠 **CY YOUNG AWARD**—The award given each year to each league's best pitcher.

🧠 *DECADES*—Periods of 10 years; also specific periods, such as the 1950s.

🧠 *DIVERSION*—Something that holds people's attention.

🧠 **EARNED RUN AVERAGE (ERA)**—A statistic that measures how many runs a pitcher gives up for every nine innings he pitches.

🧠 **EXPANSION TEAM**—A new team added when a league expands.

🧠 *LOGO*—A symbol or design that represents a company or team.

🧠 **MINORS**—The many professional leagues that help develop players for the major leagues.

🧠 **MOST VALUABLE PLAYER (MVP)**—The award given each year to each league's top player; an MVP is also selected for the World Series and the All-Star Game.

🧠 **NATIONAL LEAGUE (NL)**—The older of the two major leagues; the NL began play in 1876.

🧠 **NATIONAL LEAGUE CHAMPIONSHIP SERIES (NLCS)**—The playoff series that has decided the National League pennant since 1969.

🧠 **NL WEST**—A group of National League teams that play in the western part of the country.

🧠 **NO-HITTER**—A game in which a team does not get a hit.

🧠 **PENNANT**—A league championship. The term comes from the triangular flag awarded to each season's champion, beginning in the 1870s.

🧠 **PERFECT GAME**—A game in which no batter reaches base.

🧠 **PLAYOFFS**—The games played after the regular season to determine which teams will advance to the World Series.

🧠 *RETRACTABLE*—Able to be pulled back.

🧠 **RUNS BATTED IN (RBIs)**—A statistic that counts the number of runners a batter drives home.

🧠 **SAVED**—Recorded the last out or outs in a team's win.

🧠 **SHUTOUT**—A game in which one team does not score a run.

🧠 **SLIDER**—A fast pitch that curves and drops just as it reaches the batter.

🧠 *TRADITION*—A belief or custom that is handed down from generation to generation.

🧠 *VETERANS*—Players with great experience.

🧠 **WORLD SERIES**—The world championship series played between the AL and NL pennant winners.

EXTRA INNINGS

TEAM SPIRIT introduces a great way to stay up to date with your team! Visit our **EXTRA INNINGS** link and get connected to the latest and greatest updates. **EXTRA INNINGS** serves as a young reader's ticket to an exclusive web page—with more stories, fun facts, team records, and photos of the Diamondbacks. Content is updated during and after each season. The **EXTRA INNINGS** feature also enables readers to send comments and letters to the author! Log onto:

www.norwoodhousepress.com/library.aspx

and click on the tab: **TEAM SPIRIT** to access **EXTRA INNINGS**.

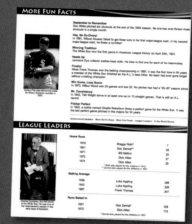

Read all the books in the series to learn more about professional sports. For a complete listing of the baseball, basketball, football, and hockey teams in the **TEAM SPIRIT** series, visit our website at:

www.norwoodhousepress.com/library.aspx

ON THE ROAD

ARIZONA DIAMONDBACKS
401 East Jefferson Street
Phoenix, Arizona 85004
(602) 462-4600
arizona.diamondbacks.mlb.com

**NATIONAL BASEBALL
HALL OF FAME AND MUSEUM**
25 Main Street
Cooperstown, New York 13326
(888) 425-5633
www.baseballhalloffame.org

ON THE BOOKSHELF

To learn more about the sport of baseball, look for these books at your library or bookstore:

• Augustyn, Adam (editor). *The Britannica Guide to Baseball*. New York, NY: Rosen Publishing, 2011.

• Dreier, David. *Baseball: How It Works*. North Mankato, MN: Capstone Press, 2010.

• Stewart, Mark. *Ultimate 10: Baseball*. New York, NY: Gareth Stevens Publishing, 2009.

INDEX

ABOUT THE AUTHOR

MARK STEWART has written more than 50 books on baseball and over 150 sports books for kids. He grew up in New York City during the 1960s rooting for the Yankees and Mets, and was lucky enough to meet players from both teams. Mark comes from a family of writers. His grandfather was Sunday Editor of *The New York Times,* and his mother was Articles Editor of *Ladies' Home Journal* and *McCall's.* Mark has profiled hundreds of athletes over the past 25 years. He has also written several books about his native New York and New Jersey, his home today. Mark is a graduate of Duke University, with a degree in history. He lives and works in a home overlooking Sandy Hook, New Jersey. You can contact Mark through the Norwood House Press website.